# CELLS OF RELEASE

# CELLS OF RELEASE

## Fiona Templeton

WRITTEN ONSITE
A CONTINUOUS LINE
A CELL A DAY

EASTERN STATE PENITENTIARY, PHILADELPHIA
APRIL 2–MAY 17 1995

INSTALLATION IN COLLABORATION WITH
AMNESTY INTERNATIONALFOR PRISON SENTENCES

*with photographs by Bill Jacobson*

ROOF BOOKS
NEW YORK

SECOND PRINTING

ISBN: 978-1-931824-73-6
Library of Congress Card Catalog No. 2018946995

The work would not have been possible without Amnesty International, and its members whose support, commitment, dirty hands and sore backs made the installation possible: Ceil Glackin in particular, and Rich Giordano, Jessica Glackin-Giordano, Jim and Donna Smith, Don Greenberg, Charles Sherrouse, Phyllis Grady, Mark Barath, Sue Mulcahy, Ruth and Dale Forney. I am very grateful to T. Kumar for his participation by writing the last cell. Thanks to Julie Courtney and Todd Gilens of Prison Sentences, Bill Bolger of the National Parks Service, Sean Kelley, Program Director of Eastern State Penitentiary Historic Site, and to Anna Kohler, Siobhan Liddell, Wendy Walker, Tom Lafarge, Eliza Jackson, Daria Fain, Carolyn Healy, Matt Smith, Jennie Shanker and the crew for their help and encouragement; to MidAtlantic Arts for a residency in Philadelphia to make the work and to MacDowell Colony where I completed the book; and to both Elaine Scarry's book, *The Body in Pain*, and Zunetta Liddell, for making me aware of Amnesty.

Parts of the text are published in Private Arts, Disturbed Guillotine and No Roses Review.

Installation photographs by Bill Jacobson.
Case photographs courtesy of Amnesty International.
Diagrams courtesy of Eastern State Penitentiary.
Materials quoted are from Amnesty publications or scraps of text found at the site.

The installation of Cells of Release is at the Eastern State Penitentiary Historic Site, at 24th and Fairmount in Philadelphia; originally created for the exhibition Prison Sentences, it will now remain open to the public when weather and building safety conditions allow, at the discretion of the site. For information contact (215) 236-3118.

**Roof Books**
are published by
Segue Foundation
300 Bowery
New York, NY 10012
seguefoundation.com

Roof Books
are distributed by
**Small Press Distribution**
1341 7th Street
Berkeley, CA 94710

*Cells of Release is dedicated to all prisoners of conscience and
victims of official violence.*

**CELLS OF RELEASE** *was an installation, created in collaboration with Amnesty International, at the abandoned panopticon Eastern State Penitentiary in Philadelphia.*

*Over six weeks, I wrote on a continuous paper that wove in and out of all the cells of one block, installing and writing one cell onsite each day. I dedicated each cell to a different current prisoner of conscience somewhere in the world, and with the old prison furniture made the cell into a place where the visitor finds a text and photograph on that case, and facilities to write in petition on their behalf.*

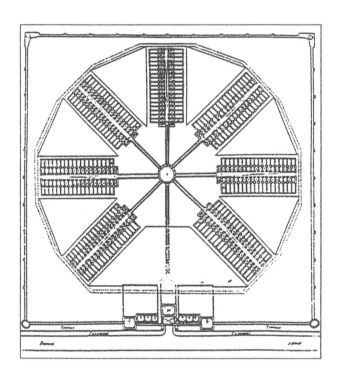

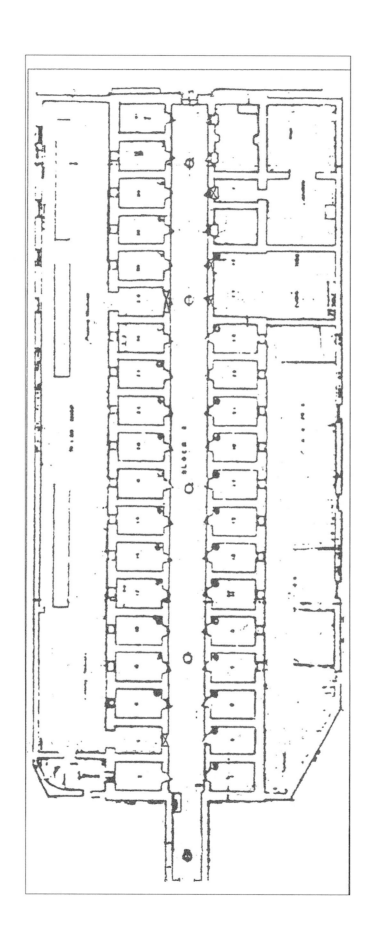

inside

where the body begins
where in begins
turns
where you are
my body
speak it
after me
sign it
with yours
unused to it
cold used
I begin inside
with you
I was afraid to begin
as if I had not
as if choice
I begin where my feet brought
or hands found
without me
a space begins
does not touch
another space
brutal and delicate
a rigid limb of cells
body parts
an empty ordering
out of me
done to
out of mind
where my body opens
skin of not body's age
white, brown
embraces the pipe to speak
or points to hollow
between the lines
to save
sense
in time
marked on me
read out
of your minding
accountable
like a mirror
right, left reversed because the numbers look back
see you
where out begins
you is a word
speak me
against nothing
a voice begins
rewrite the long arm
held against me
in evidence towards you
seen empty towards you
ends in time
outside with you
turns back inside outside
believing your choice
my onwards necessity
of wall to hours
cell per day
my days their years

slip into this hollow
surface pushes its not
your surface their not
you pushing it in
I have moved to your body
my failure keeps time
where the mind cannot hold
a poor offer but passage
or throat
and tongue
read by inside
made naked my poverty of showing
did you steal a wallet
must a pen draw blood
I have a hand in this empty cupboard
the stains on the wall are from veins of relation
cut
to shame of imagining
A man stopped at the gate the other day.  He spent fifteen years in this place, sentenced when he was a teenager.
He said, I don't think they should make museums out of what goes on in places like that.
but remembering warns us
Jacobo Timerman, Argentinian prisoner of conscience, wrote later how he hated the writer of the book that
reminded the prisoners of the existence of tenderness, and broke the barrier they constructed to survive.
so there's only the voice to give
mine
relation
these cold hands
climbing to write this
peering in darkness now
now offered to their now
this
as you read
cut now
cold now
separate now
the wall denied now
hand now
wall now
in now
body now
in now
down now
against now
through now
again now
again now
again now
again now
iron now
dust now
skin now
open now
shelf now
head now
shelf now
against now
Midas had the ears of an ass which he kept hidden under a turban.  His barber knew but Midas threatened to kill
him if he ever told the secret.  The man was desperate to say the secret so he dug a hole in the ground to whis-
per the secret into it, then filled the earth back in.  Reeds grew in that place and when the wind blew the secret
of the ears was sung across the land by the breeze playing through the hollow reeds.

I'm fighting the amnesia of this single line of time.
My mind struggles in the air for loops of relation
but when I read the other side of the doorway it says
outside with you
the wall crackles under the paper
I don't want to alter its time-drawn maps
as if connecting weren't a change
I imagine each reader bending to read
multiplying into a dance
so the voice enters the body

the you of my voice is both you, reader
and you, prisoner
the you of body
for you I continue this scratching hand even as dark comes
my world is small but I add it to yours
its voice is little but sound tonight but I say it
handle, hand on it
door, open or close
knock
refuge perverted to prison
in is also out
of the world

even the darkness here is white
a refusal to shelter
in my choice to leave, voice carried to promise
the meaning of some words must be kept
in this world
for yours
so the word you can be heard without fear
between this line and the last
a night for me
but here goes on
yes, the made is a lie of the making
between many I freeze to your image
may you enter the made to be heard
through these spaces

blue paint below green
a new prisoner
lie
the cell is empty
spits back the word prisoner in my ears
she is the one who is here at night
in case she imagines she exists
I should get down and clean the floor for you
but I want it seen for you
whose name I don't even know how to say
say to you
without an address
but my hand can copy it
your name
your name
strewing the cabinet
your name
immediate and unconditional
the terms frighten the mouth they come out of
your name
released
the line rises towards the window
for almost half your life
stand here
for almost half your life
look out to connection
killed
his body
do you even know
does body know body through walls
my mind reads the words
but some words enter my body
relationship
wallet
mouth
veil
open

hood
looking
for
closes in your face
opens like a woman
turns like a
rope
or a scarf
return release to return
restore warmth to binding
give back open to heat
turn back giving to open
restore touch to you
restore you to touch
take back meaning in your hands
woman
body
slave
target
he has the key to your door so you must be wrong
he has iron and guns so he must be strong
it's shamefully simple
where does it turn
he has the key to your door so he has the key to your door
he has iron and guns so he has iron and guns
you have your body so you have your body
in your name the exclamation mark has toppled
the body moves
the body meets
these are sounds
these are letters
the body on the page
on the line
at the door
at the thrash
hold
out

till we
hold
out
the words repeat already here between only cells 6 and 8
the words repeat but the bodies differ
Solzhenitsyn writes
There's nothing you can't do to a man.
but there it is
reduced to
do to
one does
to the other
who do
why to
open
grow
lift
eat
teach
show
feel
see
make
give
rhyme
for
with
before
as
as this darker cell comes into view

and I enter the cell
I remember writing last night that dark would be shelter
but not here
no, dark and that whole list of words only have the meaning they're given
you can take my words and recouple them with new intention
but the intention is yours
what do you intend
be quick, it's cold
I went and did some sweeping to warm up
but first
look up behind you to your left
the cells look different from the inside, don't they?
what if the door was closed?
there's the other door
to your personal yard
like a smaller cell but roofless
but you're not the one who opens that either
where would you stand in here
which way would you face
up
to the light
that was the plan
up
not to man
to connection
connection made you wrong
you'd be purified by being cut
from voice
from sight
from the gate
to the cell
you were hooded
silenced
not facing anyone
not facing
a direction
being nowhere
one was two cells away from her relative
for years

not knowing
if the other lived at all
beyond these walls
became a lie
a fiction completely in the hands of the holders
they tried to invent her meaning away
one day one world
the next another
the third another
till no world
holds
but this iron corner
it is passage that holds
as I stretch on the iron
to write passage
to intend means to stretch towards
I do not intend the iron
I will take the meaning of iron
into my hands
and change it
long pause
how, I asked myself
how will you take the meaning of iron
what is a cell of release
you are all in those spaces
that stretch
and intend
towards change
I can not mean by myself
they know this
it is their greatest weapon
more brutal than iron
which does not mean by itself
but is done to
meant to
is by someone
to someone
I stretch to
the doorway

I reach to
another doorway
nightfall
seems further
out here
up against the not a person
Once as a child I was up unusually late and caught a scene from a war drama on television. A woman was
pressed to the wall, hands stretched above her head as if trying to pull herself away from blows. A soldier flicked
a switch. She screamed a long scream and slid down the wall, her hands clawing marks. I had nightmares for
years about that wall, that the very fabric of the world could be hostile. I could not enter rooms that had that
plasterwork crafted by hand showing the sweep of fingers.

Cell 10
whose fingers are these
time
rain
neglect
and whose built what holds that surface
and whose tried to hold back
push back
push back time
before you take my meaning in your hands
time pushes by
tears by
grinds by
pounds by
burns by
claws by
racks by
ekes by
even when you turn to let it
slip by
far from you
I rose up
and disappeared
in a dream
I was still there
here
I wasn't
there
you disappeared
like magic
or murder
you disappeared like mutilation
unrecognizable
somewhere
I face away
your face away
facing me
you seem a past
they succeed
no 315
aged 13
8,000 males
70 years old
1983

mid-1970's
four complexes
four walls
two regions
two doors
two bolts
two shelves
aged 8
one lamp
28a
six bars
ten years
1995
unknown
one stool
other camps
many of them
don't count
315
solely on account
one clan
no details
no locations
no words
no word
one name
six million
no sign
no signature
one bar of soap
crumbles when I lift it
I carefully pick up all the pieces
and put them in a labelled bag
B2 C10
whose fingers
soap
against whose skin
I hold
clean paper
soiled fingers
writing my hands dirty
marking time
the stain
on the wall
looks like a face as I write my way away from it

I look back at her
saying
Oh
O
zero
none
nothing
loudly
still
tonight
tomorrow
cell
one
oh
single
oh
her
one
eye
without
out
no
else
only
to
done
no
body
315
or his
and 314
or
316
including your
one
too

looks like they dug something up in this one
will I be able to see
how far will people go in
do to
how far will people go
on
I hear the tune of an ice cream van
and I'm writing without seeing
you can't read
can't taste
can't remember
can't understand
can't please
can you wonder
can you still wonder
can you still want
ice cream
a job
an old lady
a new day
please
to please
to be used
to
slake anger
your body
your head
your neck
used to
carry
their fear
belt
whip
brick
plate
bullet
flakes of plaster
poison
lethal
legal
a written law
you can't read
do you know
do you hear
in your head
on your body
on your neck
used to
it
half your life

is not enough
to please
may I
remember
a tune
a root
growing
over
in
into a man
still a child
into a wall
into the earth
looks like they dug something up in this one
in their darkness
how far down will people go
how far will they write
their own graves
an iron door clangs in here
the wind is like footsteps
I'm afraid
and stupid
but continue for you
take you to the door
a dark rectangle
waiting
plaster falls on my head
like rain
like earth
I touch my head to feel
anything
to please
please
a good word
doesn't it say a lot
when nobody can come
about them
and say
a good word
day
ice cream
wonder
earth
dark
law
lethal
exit

saved the cut for beyond his body
yet the end like skin holds
allows bodies
allows to move
so a suture of through and exchange
coming here the car park hit me with obscenity
all those separated pods in dirt
having farted their way into rows
each curving cell tight towards itself
the more secret in the worse poison out
the surface of the earth made for their tread
not ours
their park
a numbered waiting greyer than graves
and more breathless
more little
belittled in

and in the long dark writing
in the long light shaft
in the long dark time of the cell
my particular hand
bodying its short round bursts
between each other
rubbing spark spaces
of now
a fabric to pass through
a thread to lead
little by little
not in
it's so damp
said spitting
I spoke aloud
fire under the mountain
grace
to salve abrupt union
thread of song feared
light under clod heard
try singing
for those whose songs are monstrous
against a dog set
against a naked woman
this is where my body sputters
its voice shorts
silences contort my breasts
electric
lengthening
let them only be breaths
let there still be other there
after prod
on tape
made out of broken
I can only imagine
the singing
I can't imagine
the beating
of time
out of you
I thought as I drew the needle in and out so carefully
of a vast divide
in reality
and how I hadn't yet succumbed to
had resisted
its absurdity
had refused
my cynicism
fought
my cowardice
pushed
my frustration
as if I were stronger than you
as if against remotely comparable odds
the most absurd of all
my little part
any
body's
odds
against a bursting
into
out

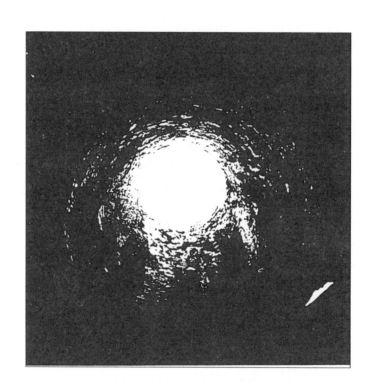

Dear Phuntsog
I hear
I can write
all the way to you
how each letter begins
dear ear
read
reach
here
priceless ear
the first name written
Robert, Zikri, Juan Antonio, Junyonto, the tumbled cry
I haven't named you into your cells
so not to hold you there
this is no memorial but of the present
to free you from the folds of a living past
even the killed are here to point the pen forwards
return the future to now
to you
I'm seeing you again
your presence
after today's activities in here
people helping
laughing
left me with

self
in the accent of my country we don't pronounce the f
take my name away
sel
in my sel
on the chest
was written
take the wire from the window
unbend it to fish in papers
put put it back
not for me to understand
fishing for clues myself
but the reader would
may never have met the writer
another writing out into
space across time
time across space
seeking reader
fish in paper
a word swims up
bakery
among the unknowable
in the item
among the unthinkable
I feel the bread betrayed in our mouths
breach of the warm body
hands in its soft belly
time pushed into its breathing
oven gaping with impunity
what word is innocent
bakery
bakery
I will hold this slash in the hearth of your image
when I go there on my way home
after stopping by
stopping
stopped

he was stopped
arrested
by an image
like a heart
arrested
ended
in the middle
from his work
to his wife
don't break, root
I won't bind you
arrested
bread in hand
seen and not seen
ended without ending
which policeman ate the bread
eight armed
and handed him
off scene
into a car
obscene
hanging unended
put put him back
take the wire from the window
unbend yoursel to fish in papers
breach the papers
a thread to lift
the burden of reading
my arms hurt with lifting
the wall is browed with moisture just above mine
a man's height in front of me
gives back no eye
or lid
nor scent
something returns
some sense
of time
this writing is of the imprint on me of the writing of the imprint on you
my body up against
the space you make through me

as the child turning in the cupboard
from dumbed blows turning
as the bird makes the nest
pushing out with its breast
turning
beside myself
curling to the wind
rolling to the wall
releasing room
for you
I prepare to meet each case
no, person
not the narrative of a symptom, of your exception
not only of cruelty and unusualness
but the body the wound replaces
living before
imagining after
the mind the wounding's world sends
blastwards

I delayed long eager to meet you
each new realer
each another stultifying me away from the door
some days picturing insults the gulf
your photo came in an envelope from an American photo store
on which was printed
memories
memories
memories
memories
memories
memories
memories
memories
memories
and across that
Treasured Moments
the moment of slipping it out
a shiny snap
as if I knew this man
prisoner 15 years
untried
untried memories
untried memories
untried memories
untried memories
untried memories
untried memories
untried memories
untried memories
untried memories
what did not happen
you are about my age
as if I had never seen America
your America an untried detention
no charges alleged
probable torture
wait

too quickly said
too easy to speak
breaks apart in my mouth
I'm returning to the door too fast
all those repeated blows of
untried
never attempted
never asked
never made difficult
never tortured
never twisted
never trodden
never turned true
never experienced
never felt in the flesh
never legal
never put to the test
never put to the tongue
never pronounced true
never tasted
never put to sense
never pronounced a person
never written
never put to the wall
never pronounced real
as if never knew this man
I never knew this man I am
but detention
stopping
holding back
keeping in
pulling from
stretching away
from reaching

held past the expiration of the sentence
squeezed after the breath has ended
kept past the useful life
continued beyond description
a voice further than breath
in after all is out
gone beyond the body's leavings
detention longer than repetition
punishment pushed out of writing
between lines of binding
embracing to death
hanging on every word
dangling from will
I must not
I must not have a will
I must not will
I will
I have not
still after your words
no charges
no moving towards
no pointing out
no hurrying to
no finger
no body to body
no law
no there
no holding to the real
no meeting
no against
only to
done
no bringing to speech
no action
no description of action
no details
no self
no cell
no place
no time
not alleged
supposed
invented
hearsay
not legal
not written to
written at
written on
not asked
probable
not said
not seen
not the first
not the only
easily
often

torture easily
torture often
twisting the rag
wringing the neck
distorting the body
doing to the tongue
breaking the real
turning the back
clenching the head
spinning the gut
weaving the arms
churning the genitals
shrivelling the lungs
corroding the eyes
souring the heart
scooping the mouth
swinging the torso
tortured moments
no memories
no memories
no memories
no memories
no memories
no memories
no memories
no memories
no memories
tightening the iron

May I mention the stress which I overcame while I was a prisoner under sentence of death? There were about 10 political prisoners who were under sentence of death in the Seoul Detention Institution. Almost all of them changed their minds and tried to give in to the dictatorial government. They strove to be granted a commutation to life imprisonment desperately. I wished to be granted a commutation too but it was out of the bounds of possibility that I could be a helper to the dictatorship. Some people have a feeling that all is vanity in life. In a sense I agree with them. But I would have no choice but to be faced with the frailty of life even if I could be granted a commutation as a result of falling away. The sense of meaninglessness of my life would bring me mental pain and exhaustion. The only way to be left to me was to walk to the execution ground with a calm manner and facial expression in peace. On the contrary those who made desperate efforts and gave in to the dictatorial government felt strong stress from the sentence of death, and became fretful and nervous. Ironically most of them died.

Is this too much too read?
If you can't read, write
I've come half way up one side of the block and can't remember what I wrote all those day week cells ago
the self part, that is
I exchanged it for your names and faces
your selves remain
wait
falter
break
I don't blame those who changed

a sweet morning in the mouth today
white violets on the way here to you
remember those
I nearly say your name like I know you
that's where the f in cell went
the locksmith told me this was the women and children's block in the 60's
maybe that's who stuck those pictures on the wall
In religious art Styka strove to convey a feeling of realism
Now the realest thing it looks like is poison
acid rotting into the sky wall behind
I saved a few broken pieces of blue and white for you
Fittingly enough, this Styka painting is in Ascension Church, New York City
something must have been rising in there
reforming up to that hole above
stuck
re-enacting abuse and trauma
emerging in you
stripped naked and made to kneel on all fours for vaginal or rectal searches at any time of day or night
controlled contained inside out
Women in general just do not go in for serious crimes, especially ones of bodily harm, of bloodshed, of violence.
Indeed for many women, life in prison literally recalls the arbitrary and self-eroding terror of life in violent rela-
tionships.
Each of the 15 individual strands of wire in the 13-foot fences bristles with 5,000 volts, 500 amperes, about 10
times the lethal dosage.
"Yeah, toast", an admiring guard in the background mutters.
Wutz fun for lil boy is death to frog
Animals wouldn't lower themselves to the level
bus graffiti this morning
remember those
bus
graffiti
lil boy
fun
after 73 years
abused to abet
now he's gone
naturally
smile of rest?
or grimace of poison in the veins today
violence all the way here to you
acid into the broken sky behind
facing
cowed from
yanked to
the legal needle
beaten to it
by him
beaten to your own
by us

violent
means becoming violet
that wasn't true till now
blood rushing to the held in
in fact violent is from the Latin word vis, meaning strength or vehemence, from the word vir, meaning a man
not the blushing shrinking
blood rushing to the held in
but words twist so easily
no sooner said than done to
word, man

here's my word on it
confinement
I looked for the roots of that, too
means having a common boundary with
the limits of the place are yours
you are cast in its likeness
into Cell 24
like Cell 22
a dress of stone
a skin of lead
a narrowing head of darkness
lung of dust
entering roots of words
the edges of your being are being weighted
what on earth are those pieces of rubble I leave you
mock earth
buried green
the edges are being charged
a drawn boundary shifts across you
not drawn by you
meaning ownership of you shifts
because borders are breached
they breach you
they cross you
and you me
I am charged with crossing
with two
I have carried another
one denies two
so says two denies one
I deny that I deny
caught out
caught in the crossfire
crossed out
a double aged
because one won
won because slaughtered
enemies are numbers
one wins
border holds
confines
but I hold in my tissue of truths
passing the language
words across limits
may I hold out
may you hold out
the walls I share an end with
the peeling finish
bounded to bound till
the limit only is mine only
where the body ends
behind you
as you cross the confines

to another word
solitary
placed apart
solo
sole
isolate
make into an island
a land in the sea
a place without other places
by itself
in its cell
shut off
insulated
secluded
excluded
lonely
abandoned
separated
not touching
not joined
solitude
sullen
desolate
make lonely
depopulate
remove contact from
remove life from
desolation
without other
not two

solitaire
a game to be played by one person
who wins
a precious stone set by itself
only
single
no spouse
to console
alone together
to comfort in distress
cut off
made powerless
made impotent
held away
at arm's length
amputated
solipsism
the theory that the self is the only object of knowledge
the lie that one is all
the lie that one is good
the lie that two is bad
the lie is to the other
and to the other of yourself
the secret is from the other
the foreigner
across a sea
across a border
across a wall
across a door
across language
across skin
across eyes
across the head
across the face
another crosses
another meets
I wanted to soften the iron bed
but the image is the lie of the real
stops me in the weaving
with pretty lies
I wanted to lay my language out for you
under you
but it's too far from your body
bodies
can speech be a body
the writing is not your husband
the writing is not your wife
the writing is not your child
though the place carries warp to my hand
I'm holding the paper between the slats
to control it
because I have no idea
I made pretty
because I have no idea
and ran home in terror
at having to say that much more
knowing nothing
reading each day more
of bodies
knowing each day less
how to speak
I am used to my own mad language
to grasp the unthought and unthinkable
repossessed from a mad world's speech
my gut has turned from irony

from artful bettering
a fabric, I thought
a repair by the hands
of home, clothing and flesh
while you need
home, clothing and flesh
but the picture turns back to a picture
I will turn to a ravening lion in your arms
but hold me
I will turn to a poisonous snake in your hands
but keep holding me
I will turn to flame in your arms
but do not loosen your embrace
I will turn to dust in your hands
but keep meaning
keep it many
keep it body
another means
I'm not in here alone
I can only do
with
I'll take blame
if you know
but I keep making
with
I'm not here to be right
I'm here to have a body
If the weaving turns trap
it's for the eyes of those entering here
to lighten the darkness
not a symbol
but this literal reflecting
in this physical cell
in Block two
in Eastern State Penitentiary
in Philadelphia
to attract the real people
this summer and fall
to go to the green desk
to read the case of real people
to pick up the given pen
and write their names
with their different hands
even those I poorly imagine
marks that carry the body to the paper
to
Dear Premier Li
becomes the you of the letter
the you turns
in your arms
in your hands
from you
till 2002

In 1989 a thin young man stood a foot in front of a moving tank, facing it, carrying a pile of strapped books and
a grocery bag.
you remember
In 1994 the U.S. President decided to extend Most Favored Nation status to China for trading.
you remember
accounting
accountable
uncounted
you count
body count

Funeral ceremony:
you
the children on the streets of Philadelphia
social undesirables and other criminals
are invited to attend your own funerals
in the near future
following elimination of undesirable elements and social cleansing
signed
the industrialists and shopkeepers of Philadelphia
whose businesses your presence is bad for
you won't miss them

Article 6.
1.
States parties recognize that every child has the inherent right to life.
2.
States parties shall ensure to the maximum extent possible the survival and development of the child.
Article 20.
1.
A child permanently or temporarily deprived of his or her family environment shall be entitled to special protection and assistance provided by the State.
Article
a thing said
a moveable thing

my grandmother's worst insult
ye article
she possessed little
but not as little as this
a room not fit for a thing
a dead body
in old Irish cel means death
we've called a cell life
but we really mean a separateness
I followed the word back
to a hut
in Sanskrit sola
a place to hide
insideness
a hall
a sheath
a cave
an enclosure
hollow
hole
cellar
the dungeon of language where I rummage for the turning of the word
hull
hulk
hell
colour conceal helmet
ciliary
like an eyelash
shuts the eyes away
shuts the face away
the helmet is not the person
not a person
inside against
clam
secret
silent
clandestine
by analogy with intestine
insides in
in the open
in is different to out
a change of meaning
is a change of heart
let in not be out
let them remain different
but private is not locked by another
choose
locked into one place
or locked out of all
all prospect no refuge
all journey

the stations of it
moving
and it all starts again
where you want to lie
you get up
falls for the second time
till you lie nowhere
shut out
shut in
shut up
shut down
the body on the side walk
is clammed from our eyes
nothing to see with
is french for nothing to do with
nothing to say with
but letters

isn't this a nice cell
green is my favourite colour
I painted my apartment like this
but I have nothing to do with
not interested in saying self
held in the speech bubble
pointing back to
but in singing
saying to
or making
though wearied by litany
looking
all absent and correct
right
correct
correction
rectitude
rectify
right reich reign rex regal regiment region royal
regular regulate rule
direct direction address dress
erect adroit
redress rich reach
right?
straight
upright stretched
lying standing
not gauche
not sinister
not different
not curved
correction makes straight
a clean cut
direction commands
is two
a region is made by lines
dividing
the rectum is the straight part of the intestine
straight through
clean through
nothing incorrigible
all absent and correct
not twisted
not tortured
not immobile
a straight line
is the fastest way
to correct
counteract
neutralise
chastise
amend
fix
make into sticks
remove the fat
shave the bones
straight as a rule
as die
when you wish for a less torturous way

I had chosen these cells near each other for metaphoric connection
starving to death
and being beaten so hard his intestines were forced out through his anus
but sometimes bringing these obscenities out
seemed as obscene as doing to the body
lower than toilet scrawls
in their need
but I know there's need here too
it's private but it mustn't be a secret
turning the inside out
and denying the inside
facing outside in
like the clawmarks on the wall
come alive with death
an outside in of people
a negative
a no
no
pain is no
I had thought I'd be dealing with a simpler out and in
incarceration
isolation
but who severs the invisible links will sever the flesh
this is more than a picture
a person is perceptible and perceiving
but pain is not a thing
it is no in the body
but can you see if it has the shape of at least the body
when all else falls away
stripped away
forced away
not that metaphor can be pain or match it
why double it?
but that speech articulates the cry
lets it move
there is neither special metaphor nor lack of it in the language of fact
a fact is thing made
nor in the language of the subject
the one who experiences
the second has a place
a context
the context may be a cell
and if this writing is a speech of neither in nor out
a frame running through
may it register the doubling
wincing off the walls
keeping on in and out

a theatre of memory and now
making visible this their time
your now
whose line is for the body to read
and say at least
"said"
and for the foldings to meet later
the binding sits echoing
healing private
if healable
or is this me reopening
the wound to forage
scavenge
I tried to take apart language
looking for reason
but again it sprawls dismantled
impotent and ashamed
reason meaning motive
why
intent in the two-facedness of words
or value
it all gets back to body count
even one body
yes or no
isn't she lucky
to be raped in custody
so doesn't have to prove
that she didn't say yes
in custody
in care
doesn't yes the didn't yes
come in
I am in
you are over
signs of resistance
movement crushed on this floor
traces you
I dragged myself here
after a break
in the wall of only this
the wall reared again
I was terrified of coming back here
the choice revealed the painfulness
I began to understand why Timerman hated the tender
though I'd thought that a woman
I
couldn't conceive of survival without it
against the having to
done to
a turn
tenderness
but then I went out and felt some
or even imagined it
and something broke
inside
against a floor

I'd been yearning for a break
as in dam
or fever
or into fever
out of reason
wanting my tongue to fork
but I have to go to hell first
into the blinding
down to not
no me not body
forgetting how I know
but sure as in nightmare I knew

I stripped speech naked to discover why to respect it
threw away elsewhere to look for where I am
trying to have no tongue to trip on
becoming breathless
speech dry as intention alone
thinking it can wash over me
lucid with treachery
banal with one man's meat
abstract with wishing
straight to hell
by a process of elimination
myself behind
an excluded language
you inside
out of the picture
a language from which is excluded
a society of cuts
a code of hells
again I'd thought what I'd mean in here
but the meaning of saying has changed
there is no language of all our mouths
it's all found in the translation
across sides
covering the head
and as I unbuilt and undressed
to imagine into
she in the body's worst
had imagined out
where imagination remained
remnant
tatter
veil
darkly
refrain
my attempt a useless weapon across the face
stinking of joyless
across a two-faced
affronting
so this is how I talk of woman child custodial rape
of opening or closing the veil
of faces made unseeable
mouths made unspeakable
I can't get close
I'm leaving again
the being in the world of these women

becoming object and instrument
in the hands of ordinary
ordinary
soft
invisible
disfigured
beautiful
breached
vulnerable
silenced wherever they can open
straighten the trickle
straighten the lips
make a man of
make a woman of
the straightest way in
relate
join
relate
tell
and I've bared what I thought I wouldn't
so let the room speak

I aim the pen to the telling again
and can't write those words
to read this close to the skin
I'm shaking this close to the moisture
the small hairs
the membrane
in the time of skin to skin holding
how
the very lip in the very fingers
held
this gap
this time
this blank
space of infinitesimal articulation
of the hand before the mark
between curved and straight
between form and spill
between agreement and will
between relation and thing
hand held as if to avowal
to signature
under pain of
under pain of sense
must turn to itself
inside returns sense
to itself
returns senses
eye to eye
speaks back
looks up
looks up
speaks out
message
passage
message
passage
message
passage
mouth into mouth
tongue to ear
handed back
from here at the innest of the body
without altering its course
at the boundary of the world
where the downwards
climbs
from here in hell
at the boundary of the body
where the inwards
replies
plies its way
reply your sense
of space
of touch
curves
cups
catches
whispers back
refrains

breathes again
stood for a week before blood and number
echoing
refrains
tongue naked
falls
into the body to body
flouted afoul down their arms
never told why
mental health or otherwise
denied my identity
I was banned
if moved
never told how long
burning
soles
dragged out
of lights
of a taut wire
pull it up with your
field of clover
sewn screaming
to be split
how to say be
where
beg out of the ghosthouse
transferred to the minefield
there are no such thing as ghost houses
crushed by a soul
tank in
day out
with plastic piping
with a heavy sharp tool
from eating
from praying
bad things
unidentified
and his brains were
disqualified
all over the wall

wound
secret in the thorax
and that's it
my elder brother
made a video
her husband and brother in law
no such thing
solely for allegedly
was in no shape
to be dressed for the other side
family and friends
smashed with a blunt
by the wedding ring he wore
held in the basement of Vartek's department store
women's section the next day at a Zagreb rubbish dump
in his native language
no doings
done
whereabouts and grounds
unable to control near a restaurant
bag of clothes
nothing
cowdung disfiguration
concrete swelling
cobweb children
never handed over
on our arms
a hot policy
in his chest
I was lashed
it affected me
morals crossed behind their necks
the rubbish you are wearing
defines a terrible throe

disadvantaged is forbidden
by the IMF
my soul is aimed
would totter
carrying buckets of
chest, arms, belly, back, kidney and legs
I reacted
SPLA
JNA
WC
WB
Please give my watch to the World Bank
give my stench
one of the heart
sight, hearing, several teeth

led
in the head
out of the world
unearthed
chained naked
put on public
forced to write and sing all night
hacked
I myself was lined up
belts around
banged against
polarised
like sardines in a can
like dogs out of a tin
Khartoum rained blows
sons
a travesty of each other
of saying
Croatian findings on the river bank
Indian dead rights in her arms

been
had been
were
verbal and innocent in the passage or bathroom
cleansing
simply copies of
your underwear
of your country
beating and then treating
have been
is being
were
are
done to
of lice
bigger
of committing

of crawling
towards a source of light
an ear
a cold ceramic curl
hold body's internal image
toilet bowl told dry
this is not a secret
between bodies
this is not a threshold
between bodies
no tread
at the limit of consciousness

this is not held
a laid noose
to arm you
a rope of tongueing
in time
a torsion to mark
to hold out
light to a dark coil
keep sense
by saying beyond
in the wrong language
spit elsewhere
imagining what a voice might be
doing what you can wrench
I had chosen this room for you
when I heard that the 12 year old Pakistani boy I had first chosen it for had been released
he had been under death sentence for blasphemous graffiti
although he was illiterate
the room is larger than the other cells
a mockery of a house for you
the boy is released
but has to hide
he reports that he wishes he could go out and play
like a normal boy
arrested by hate
your house arrest
arrested by your own house
country
what is a kitchen for?
would one person alone have invented a knife?
in how many directions can you face?
on the other side of this cell block
I wrote less harshly on the exterior walls
on this side of the block I've written cruelty on the outside
and am softening in here for you
Siobhan installed this cell
she chose it
not knowing which case would be here
her grandmother was Burmese
her sister Zunetta wrote the Human Rights Watch report on Burma
they have shown me their grandmother's silk
what hangs on your walls?
does it show that they have cruelty written on the outside?
Siobhan did not hesitate to bring beauty into this cell
we do what we can turn
the paper is lips and arms
hair and loop
Rapunzel to the inside
and to a source of light
bathes and binds
as far as its self is possible
where does a body end
on the inside
a rod in its core
made into made to make softness hold
hold the tread
to a turning
beauty turns
at the limit of consciousness
and holds
at the belly of gravity

at the centre of the body
there is a holding stronger than the surface of the earth
there is a breathing through walls
you have chosen the walls on the inside of your country
rather than those that surround it
ministering to the interior
your body is a voice
and the walls by their presence speak back
that they are no mouth to step through
a body takes place
happens
changes
prisons are less place
disappeared is even less place
let beauty take place
dead is no place
food, clothing, shelter and place
a country is a place
a place touches other places
places loop, cross, lap, turn, open
places are what take place
what is a bedroom for
urine and curry powder in the flesh slit with bamboo
are what touch
what place
take place away
please
take body away
take the place of me
you can not take their place
their place takes you
it is taking you most of yourself
in the name of the place
it was nine forearms deep
the top was just big enough for one person to go through
I had to be supported by two men in order to be able to move
he was unable to speak
released because he was no longer able
beaten because they were not able
I was speaking to one while I was able
but numbers I can only speak of
killed I can only
forced to work as a porter knocked unconscious
systematically fractured
secretly cremated
I noticed dark marks
I prepared a new game
who were our contacts
held in the dust
what sort of activities
kneeling on glass
who was leading
covered with a plastic bag
called having a bath
called the motorcycle
the helicopter
fan belt
wet scalp
submarine
heavy log
behind the golf course
by the pond

what are you worried about
drumstick
rice bag
leave me alone
paralyzed by the objects' own amnesia
numbed with number
million
silence is not a countable noun

responsible people don't just go around hollering genocide
said Ambassador Rawson
if
if they'd hollered genocide about Rwanda the US would have been obliged to act
according to the treaty drawn up 50 years ago that promised
never again
even if a state department memo at the time interpreted obliged as enabled

if
if the original Belgian colonists hadn't justified their colonization of the already complex Rwandan society, since they couldn't claim they were civilizing it, by identifying the Tutsi administrative class as Hamites or Black Aryans, maybe it would still have been possible for Hutu to become Tutsi, as before

before somebody hollers genocide
somebody else has hollered different
with hate
if
if the World Bank hadn't forced a new economic and agricultural system on Rwanda of pseudo-western
capitalism, maybe corruption at the top and misery at the bottom wouldn't have been guaranteed
hollering different

just hollering
hollering is a countable noun
you
and you
ignorance is thinking it's not to be thought
or written
somebody who came by the other day asked
so are you hoping people might read some of the stories
maybe even think about something they feel connected to?
well, I suppose the people who built this place hoped it would keep people in
no, that's a bad analogy
force and resistance
or
I suppose if someone asks that question I'd be presumptuous to assume persuasion
this one's glasses are really cool
this one's just a kid
but looks shifty
what do people have in common after all
besides body and consciousness
or besides body
the same person asked if I thought there were ghosts in here
he thinks dead people are scary?
he should read
well, maybe he should look at pictures
he said you should have things for people to take away
oh right
things
for people to take away

they saw in the dim light the headless figure facing them
with a crust of bread in one gloved hand
and a chunk of cheese in the other
that's him
said Hall
what the devil's this
came a tone of angry expostulation from above the collar of the figure
you're a damned rum customer, mister
said Mr. Jaffers
but 'ed or no 'ed
the warrant says body
and duty's duty
he would stand trial for provoking trouble
he would be tried as a Vietnamese delinquent
and not as a Buddhist
for protesting against the law that orders young monks to register for military service
and duty's duty
he should read
is this a story?
maybe he should look at pictures
the warrant says body
what do people have in common
faint and transparent as though it were made of glass
so that the veins and arteries and bones and nerves
could be distinguished
the outline of a hand
a hand limp and prone
it grew clouded and opaque even as they stared
and so beginning at his hands and feet
and creeping along his limbs to the vital centres of his body
that strange change continued
first the little white nerves
a hazy grey sketch of a limb
then the glassy bones and intricate arteries
then the flesh and skin
first a faint fogginess
then growing rapidly dense
presently they could see his crushed chest
and the dim outline of his drawn and battered features

at last there lay
naked and pitiful on the ground
the bruised and broken body of a young man
and his eyes were like garnets
the hands were clenched
and his expression was one of great dismay
Cover his face
said a man
Cover that face
for people to take away
things for people
left here

                    things left
                   out of stories
                      people
                        left
                  in the selves again
                     I also found
                   cut-out heads
                     of all sizes
              arranged facing each other
             and in heated conversation
                     says body
           how the shape of him says body
                     by edges
            how the edges of the cells blur
                     in saying
            how the edges of selves blur
                  in conversation
                       edged
                     to please
                     to move
               in thousands of letters
                     by name
              at least we have a name
                  for the shape
                   body or body
                  it is unclear
                 so it seems real
              as if from a photograph
                     traced
                at least your trace
                     cut out
                   from place
        in a shape of doing or standing at least
           but then cut out from the inside
                 leaving no doing

no standing
only not being
noplace
the bodiless figure
held
and knowing held away
in a closed society
it is virtually impossible
to verify the government's claims
that the individual named
is not in detention
or may constitute
a threat to closure
that is, security
so perhaps that strange shape is a good way to represent you after all
where you have your body
but elude its enclosure
in yourself
virtually impossible to verify
few facts to falsify
no charges
but you do have your body
against what edges now
what lying on
what standing on
what held against
how fast
how repeatedly
how hard against
how long against
what edge against
what change against
what person left

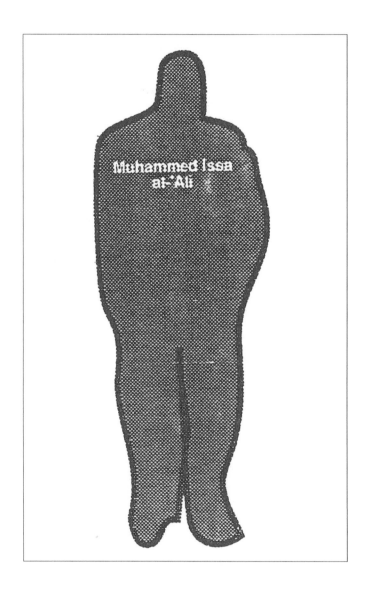

as I leave this cell
as others leave
not to leave you
but to leave for you
all the entering and leaving for you
an open door
but leading to another
which I'll also leave
for people to leave
a big centipede
in the dark
I do want to leave
what do we have in common?

it's gone
I meet so little life here
it must have gone into a crack
between edge and edge
living
in one of the corridor walls there's a piece of hair hanging out
that looks like my hair
reddish
like the centipede
and here I am
down on the ground
near hard edges
and cracks
thinking about Conchita Bajao
When you're being beaten
there's the pain
immediate
there's that your body
and you can't think of much else
is penetrable
open edges
forced entry from anywhere
not you-shaped
that you're a thing
an anything
an else
it would be better to be the door against which
and you try to
there's that this anything-making of you is a person
a you
like you
now not like you-not-you
now like what
which is the person?
you're not you
but nobody else
or nothing else you know
that you taste the world and yourself
dust and blood
acid out of your stomach and something you come into

comes into you
wood
plastic
stone
they're insider and outsider than you know
they're together
they're now
they're what you know
and sight
between opening eyes to save
and closing eyes to save
corners closeups reversals
you're try to hang onto
because you're trying to hang on
know up
know exposed
know out
but no time
but more now
and no choice
and you're saying as you see
automatically in your head
floor
just to not only say no
not even say but be
not be no
and not understanding
but needing to at least understand
and so from yourself
as having some kind of direction toward
and not only to
not-you done to
some hope that things link
not just smash
because if you can't get it
you can't imagine else or after
so fear in the only now
of only now ever
now being not you
no link
pain, immediate

no link because to be in the world you can't think this possible
because then it's any time possible
because no reason you know now
and fear too that there is a reason
that this happens and will
and you are the reason
but you have no direction towards this
none of any of this is thinking
and all for a way out of your body
which is pain
to find your body
which you can't remember
or were mistaken about
till now

and if you know the person
less link
no person possible
all link broken
on your head
Art use
one ni
Franklin R
ving unem
a giant buck
way from the
tic.  A drunk
we don't," He
or that
it." Fo
him or n
I can st
sorry he
funny
sin
con
bad
lik
th
broken with time
words curling away
from paper pasted
to the side of the desk
writing side in
I read it after falling
in Cell 21 last night
I'd had one foot on the desk
the other foot on the chair
which toppled as I wrote
"know up"
I brought it here
for you to read
please don't break it further
see how I fell into the bottom shelf

you don't know these people
and to you it's a strange language
but lucid
when left with room
to imagine
it doesn't take much
speech side out
from speech side in
NDEHURIO
from irregularities
obtain and publish
from proscribed area
release
from arrest
without breaking
the body
away

gone
missing
missed
wanted
wanting
lacking
not here
elsewhere
nowhere
where
disappeared
vanished
lost
omitted
from home
inexistent
flown
nobody
void
beyond
cleared
not of this world
transparent
inaccessible
out of the way
poof!
alien
inconsequent
inapplicable
lapsed
segregated
far-fetched
abstract
who cares
out of mind
left out
get out of here
ejected
rejected
excreted
vomited
wasted
swept aside
struck off
neither here nor there

unsaid
disembowelled
beat it
extracted
drained
wrung out
devoured
plucked
given away
refused
to the dogs
out of the question
Xed
trashed
dried up
redundant
jettisoned
ceased
terminated
rid
unwanted
subtracted
removed
stolen
ebbed
shunted
abducted
repelled
absent
offed
no trace
hence
bereaved
sequestered
possessed
engulfed
culled
negated
killed
stopped
disallowed
reaped
shrunk to nothing
a hole
out of body
without so much as a goodbye

released
would bring body
goodbye
and the body brings
when I leave this place
it is as if it has poisoned the world
the buildings of power are sick with holding
their shape is evil with meaning
not nice old history
this building says fortress
war
blood
boiling oil

killing for having
as all killing is
when wanting turns holding
it excludes
a prison is a grip
an embolic heart
I stopped my day at that thought
of countries too
but come back
and go on
towards your need
I feel like I'm writing a tunnel
daily
writing a vein
writing a lung
coming and going
one breathing
of breaths
the day is the beat
but who bends their ear to their own heart?
sometimes freedom is doing that
sometimes necessity
I hear Homer's music from the next block
no silence for the one who can't leave
the coming and going
of the head on the wall
deafened by days
my mind is harder to bring to you
I speed
in dismay
from you at the heart
of the cell I hardly hear
you're the ones I should bring

this tripping complete syntax rides waves of wrong world
out
learning a language for the body but not of it
I never imagined I'd want to slow down here
the air in this talking is too thin
seethru
I wanted to vise the tress
catch and pull you
and another body will follow
another hand
a chain of chains
links need space
to catch
to pass

I almost passed this other marking
hatching in the doorway
broken but made
and though not decipherable
somehow understandable
I don't understand
the keeping to break
prison
prae-hendere
to seize before you
hold in
hand
get
a prey
prise
apprehend
pregnable
reprisal
get back
misapprehension
getting it wrong
get him wrong
got him wrong, abi
and the darkness did not comprehend it
surprised
overtaken
taken over
reprehensible
held in check
held guilty
grasped on your head
be it
seize to account
run away
ran away from his mother who held
apprehension
apprentice
master
held accountable
browbeaten
head in hands

capital punishment
blaming by head
revenge on the head
Abdullah mentally subnormal after
Robert significantly retarded before
"If the law regarded life as inviolable, then the people would begin also so to regard it.  A deep reverence
for human life is worth more than a thousand executions in the prevention of murder.  The law of capital
punishment, while pretending to support this reverence, does in fact tend to destroy it."
While almost every other country in the developed world, so-called, has abolished the death penalty, the
number of US states that allow the death penalty is increasing steadily.
This week the state of Alabama reintroduced the chain gang.
The only other countries in the world that have carried out as many executions as the US are Iran and
Iraq, where they also brand people.  Is cutting off a hand less reverential of the body than killing it?
Capital means head
is aimed at the head.
I came back to this cell
to join your body to those of other children
but who have more legal hope of life
your head
is drawn
a line around
keep it
on
appeal
and on
and on
repeal
The US carries out more executions of juveniles than almost any other country in the world.
The execution of people under 18 at the time of the crime is expressly forbidden under international law,
including agreements to which the US is signatory, although the US has as yet failed to ratify the
International Convention on the Rights of the Child.
the head of a child
falling in the grip
the head of a child
in the hands of this country
does not understand
I don't understand
a death penalty case
costs several times more money
than life imprisonment
because of legal fees
for appeal
and on

I can't imagine
held sorry and fixed
a girl in here
is reading a magazine
found here
a blue
clamshell shaped
bar
dominates one corner
of the large room
its surface
is of milkglass
surrounded by a rim
a hundred pieces of foam
covered in patent leather
in the background
are the pair of chrome ball chairs
that absorb the sitter
a girl absorbed
in a chair
absorbed
in punishment
taken up
ball and chair
gone in the chair
a sunburst mirror
is placed in the entryway
to reflect the mood
of the dramatic choice of furnishings
a dining table
set for guests
a conversational island
for talking to yourself
there are no shelves
only revolving lazy susans
only Ayat turning
and the master baths
rhodocrysite
and 14-carat gold
the room is capable of accommodating parties
of at least one
hundred
an array
of lucite lamps
chromed ashtrays
steel sculptures
bathed
in points of light

visitor receipt
house of correction
the sum specified is received this date for credit to the account of
date received 5 11 71
prisoner's number
$5
send a generous sample of your hair
taping both ends of hair sample with Scotch tape
you'll look lovelier instantly
eliciting painful burns in the eyes

The procedure to follow when the phone rings is
raid the community
answer phone immediately and
break into the house without a search warrant
wait till originator of call identifies himself and postand order all the family members together in one spot
and give reason for alarm
accuse them of being guerrillas
this message will be repeated continuously
and the mother and older children will be interrogated
until all posts have received message
under threats and ill-treatment
upon signal of caller
hit the children
or officer in charge
threaten to rape Yajaira
all phones will be hung up
and father and son will suffer brutal torture
at the count of three
I will twist the language at least twice
with an unknown substance
all of this writing is here
those who asked the questions were hooded
those who were questioned were semi-suffocated with plastic bags containing ammonia
neither doer nor done to have faces
those who are done to have names
the doers none
between the actions there can be no spaces
wait till originator of call identifies himself
signs
upon himself

Holdings
name of account
security name
face amount of shares
based on 1967 year end prices
Audit report
name of account
residence Philadelphia
guardian
Chip a Roos bunkhouse
Assignments
search ordered
Great gifts for Dad
men's ruffled shirts

My daily life is monotonous and changeless.
There are only two men,
I and a prison guard.
I wonder which foreign language is the most useful
in leading a life internationally
and making friends.
The toilet in my room is not a flush toilet
but I am not as lonely as in Andong Prison.
Sultry heat keeps on far into the night.
Writing this letter I am dripping with sweat.
I received packages with watercolour with thanks.
A political prisoner in another cell is in those days lost in drawing pictures
He was beside himself with joy.
I hope you to send me the next time
a few pieces of Ivory soap
and what I can have with relish.
It is really a happy imagination
that I will be seated in your kitchen
and have some baked bread.
The temperature drops below zero.
My room which has no heating is so small
that I can make the air of my room warm with my body heat
and the stream of my health.
Poor conditions of a prison
prevent prisoners who have lived in prison for a long time
from having good health.
When I wake up
the water in the pail in my room has been frozen.
May I ask you a favor?
I need a world map.
I hope to attach it to the wall of my room
and learn English names of places by heart.

these are the words of another from your country
but I gave them to you
because you have none
I need a new map of the world too
with the names of the places called differently
will I find it by my sel one
the last cell where I wanted to leave the dirty rags
because cloth touches skin
in another life
in a respoken world
a map of passing

when everything takes
something gives
but I'm nearing the hub again
the base of the finger
the eye in the heart of control
of the ring of spikes
these are not the cells of a body
not active
but swallowed other
held undealt
like this mouth of hair and dust
in the wall above me
bound but divided
like a country
word and meaning
I haven't spoken of the one who was born in prison and lived there till the age of 17
not just an outside dreaming an outside
but a during dreaming an after without a before
and an after I can not even dream of
as if this writing knew no elsewhere
had no meaning for release but not
though I've tried to have no delete function
no seamless dropping through
because there is no such thing as disappearance
but I had my elsewhere to go to
and what would my silences be
or my refrains
if there were no elsewhere to know them
or to come and hear
if the only elsewhere was here too
a prisoner is a scapegoat
a sin-eater
who ate the sins
to take them away
is taken away
so you can be clean
but the goat at least escaped
here there is no erasure
but an erosion
a stammering
a toll on the real
a nowhere if place is relation
but a travelling from mouth to ear
if it is heard
if your beautiful name is read

how can the desire of not be told
resisted some cells to rewrite them
but failed in some cells to invent not them
but let each step break open
and failures be room
recording now to represent not now
repetition resembles but repetition of the single can't tell
and free doesn't mean doesn't cost
cost is exchange
and the real costs the real
body costs body dear
held dear
dear held

Dear Victoria Zumaeta Arista
Estimada Sra Victoria Zumaeta Arista
He aprendido un poco de su historia
por los medios de Amnistia Internacional
Aunque no hablo muy bien espanol
le estoy escribiendo a vd
para decirle
los sentimientos
de una mujer extranjera
Aun no se si el espanol es su lengua
ni cual idioma vd habla
pero tanto mas no puedo imaginar su vida en el carcel
Espero que vd sea bien tratada
y que llegue a ver a sus ninos y a su familia
Su encarceracion me parece una injusticia
y que vd deberia estar libre a tener las opinionas que quiere
y a decirlas
Ninguna persona tiene la derecha
de maltratar el cuerpo de otra persona
estoy comunicando su situacion a otra gente
y estan escribiendo para pedir su libertad
la libertad del cuerpo
y del hablar
No se que mas decirle
pero le envio la simpatia
por su situacion muy dura
espero que vd tenga buen salud
y coraje
Yo soy escritora
pero lo mas claro
es escribir para vd

but the clearest
I am a writer
you were washing clothes
Pienso a vd lavando ropa
cuando le tomaron
when they took you
Pensare a vd
when I do the same
cuando yo hago lo mismo
for you
Pardon my faults
if this is your language
If any language
then saying what?
take my pen

A GROUP OF PRISON GUARDS CAME TO MY CELL.
NEEDLESS TO SAY I WAS NERVOUS.
ARE THEY GOING TO TORTURE ME?
I HAD ENOUGH.
THE GUARDS CHECKED MY PRISON NUMBER AND NAME.
THEN THEY TOOK ME OUT OF THE CELL.
I WAS TAKEN BEFORE THE HEAD OF THE PRISON.
HE INFORMED ME THAT THE GOVERNMENT HAS DECIDED TO RELEASE ME.
I WAS THRILLED.
THRILLED TO BE A FREE PERSON.
I THOUGHT OF THE PEOPLE AND ORGANIZATIONS THAT WORKED TIRELESSLY FOR MY RELEASE.
ONE GROUP ATTRACTED MY SPECIAL ATTENTION.
A GROUP OF PEOPLE I NEVER MET.
YET THEY WORKED MY RELEASE.
THEY ARE THE MEMBERS OF AMNESTY INTERNATIONAL.
PEOPLE FROM DIFFERENT COUNTRIES, DIFFERENT CULTURES, WORKING FOR A COMMON GOOD.
THE PEOPLE WHO NEVER KNEW EACH OTHER.
BUT HELPING FOR THE SAKE OF COMMON GOOD.
THE UNKNOWN HELPING THE UNKNOWN.
MY HEART WAS FILLED WITH GRATITUDE FOR THESE UNKNOWN PEOPLE.
MY THOUGHTS ALSO WENT ABOUT MY FRIENDS WHO DISAPPEARED.
THOSE WHO WERE TORTURED AND THOSE WHO ARE STILL IN PRISON.
I WAS TAKEN TO THE FRONT GATE.
THE GUARDS SHOOK HANDS WITH ME.
A RARE OCCURRENCE IN THE PRISON.
THE HEAD OF THE PRISON ACCOMPANIED ME TO THE DOOR.
NO NIGHTSTICKS, NO DOGS, NO HANDCUFFS.
ABOVE ALL, LEAVING A PLACE FOR A VERY LONG TIME.
AS I STEPPED OUT I SAW MY FRIENDS WHO WERE WORKING WITH ME TO FIGHT INJUSTICE.
CHEERING CROWDS OF STUDENTS REMINDED ME OF THE STRUGGLE TO WHICH I WAS PART OF.
THE PRISON MAY HAVE DELAYED THE STRUGGLE
BUT IT SURE DID NOT STOP ME.
THE TIME IN PRISON HELPED ME TO REALISE THAT
STRUGGLE FOR JUSTICE IS THE MOST REWARDING EXPERIENCE A HUMAN BEING CAN HAVE.
THE PRISON AND THE RELEASE ALSO HELPED ME TO REALISE THE BASIC TRUTH.
NO MATTER WHERE WE COME FROM WE ARE ALL MEMBERS OF THE HUMAN FAMILY.
AMNESTY INTERNATIONAL IS THE PROOF OF THIS TESTIMONY.
THE STRUGGLE STILL CONTINUES.

so that the body continues
so that the voice continues

outside

# Notes on making
## CELLS OF RELEASE

*Before the visitor interprets, she has brought her body. And in order for the visitor to perceive, the body goes further still, accompanies the work. The installation is an accommodation, gives place to the cases. Often, the reading visitor unconsciously entered the dance of detail, while the seeing one held back unbodied in the whole, the work's gesture got, apart. Who saw "sad stories" sees them as finished, because not himself, rather than as able to include himself, his gesture. In some ways the narratives are hardly stories (we think fictional?) but bodies, so particular, skin-bounded, but also human, so similar, and now, so incomplete. The body of the case has the potential to be made whole by another's, the visitor's. Some are closed but here to be opened, to the air; some are open wounds to heal. In the healthy body, a cell releases in recognition; but while it does not encounter what it perceives as other to itself, it remains inactive and vulnerable.*

*Like ritual, like exercise, like pilgrimage, like dance, though made simply to experience or for the body, the visitor's walk reinscribes links on time, on body. The balk, shiver, sigh or shrug, the choice to go partially, these too repeat, pattern time. The signature is action and act, points back to the body, (ac)countable in. The walk multiplies name and names. And leaving, turns inside out.*

*On continuous paper with an indelible marker, I wrote without the possibility of erasure or retrace. Where a spool of paper ran out, I sewed on the next one. A single prison sentence. So writing both committed, and was always forwards, time's two-way burden. To have the writing participate in every cell gave myself no way out of the quantity, to do time, doing as active. And my necessary failures are vulnerable, uncomfortable, imperfect. But of course my narrative was also thus bounded by place, its boundedness to make bearable the vastness of its matter repeated in countless bodies. The release that the second half of the work knows it heads for after the hell of the first facing, is the present fiction. But it ends with a true story, T. Kumar's, a former prisoner of conscience in Sri Lanka and now living in the U.S., who wrote the last cell, story, which yet opens beyond his own happy ending. The closure had to open. What clangs or gapes behind? Just as the work needed to be handed over at the end, it also needed the empty unwritten cell at its center. The unsayable that was nevertheless done, by a body to a body. But not at the end; the action of writing out had to begin again after that. Writing out: what the body does even when not invention. Sometimes I could only copy, standing on a stool contorted to the looping line.*

*It is hard to represent on the pages of a book the physical continuity of the original writing. I felt mostly the single journey that I was making and a reader might, the links I was trying to weave at least concretely out of the separated. The breaks and new beginnings of pages are often false to my dailiness; often that was interrupted by my turning to face a new view into or out of a cell, or a scribble on a wall; often I could write no longer in darkness or cold or damp; often I was overwhelmed by my subject matter and my relation to it or lack of means of writing it. But the centralizing of the phrases one above the other on the page is familiar as the block's symmetry, that of the cell, of the central observation tower, and of the body.*

*Harder still to imagine on the page, perhaps, is the strange linearity of the writing that lost its past, went only on, structured only by the very physical awareness of repeated enterings and leavings, which seemed respectively single and general, and the long downward inward movement to the end of the block and up back out. Inside the cells my mind would circle reduced, looking for imagination but stubbing on the walls, the facts, yet again, yet again. I could hardly keep myself in. The corridors stretched away, scale, the many, the walk. The writing probably says it.*

*I was at an edge again, between wanting to see what happens to the writing, up against where silence used to be prescribed, but has now become guilty; and to see if the matter itself could be infused with the seeing-anew of art, not to alter the matter but to turn activity to it. I am under no illusion that either is justified by the other; if anything I hope for a productive friction. Where the bounded, the artifice and the represented meet the sticky or invasive, the accidental, the remade-present, there also meet the specific body/ies and the shifting multiple subject (rather than the self); in time as well as the more obvious place. In this between are asked the questions: of art as hermetic or relative; of whether it is possible to understand (or admit) another's subjective experience and its difference, and whether art can materialize that; of what a human can do in relation to another's body, or not. Art and body both are matter.*

*But daily, repulsion and attraction, will and viscera, a frighteningly small loop of reaction and language. Hence the* repetition, in context a hanging on desperately, but on the page, repetition. Or a hammering away at something, trying to worry (as a dog does) my way out of it. I also hated finding myself at the center of it. That wasn't the point and exacerbated the ethical riddle. That was on the first side, going down into, trying to get past my own difficulty. On the second, scrabbling in a rage of body parts, scraps of language, tricking myself from the difficulty, to materiality (part of the difficulty), lulled in exhaustion, to get out.

And I could be caught into beauty too. The metaphor of the woven bed meant all the more paper, more to write; the photogenically distressed walls were slow poison, the dustmask hard to keep on for hours. Where began drawing attention and ended distracting, between horror and making? There's been a time when all art seemed to me violence because forging place out of none, just as all naming bloody because separating, possessive. Of course such qualities are each at an extreme of making or of naming. But to write on, for example, torture, I walked these scales.

Writing on place is less abstract than on the mobile book. It was an irony I saw later that in searching for a less volatile writing I had turned two huge iron locks on it (literally—for weeks the only person in the building, I had to lock myself in). And that I also put the writing into an environment where it would slowly perish. In cell 36 I knew that as I broke my head to imagine in, "she in the body's worst" imagined out. This is why, though bitter others' writings dissuaded me, I did want to make in there. Struggle has to wish for its own end. So though fearful, play was more than avoidance, and beauty need too, lightness to handle and lift. Detached, perhaps that writing can bring place with it. (Perhaps; I hadn't written for the book's reader to feel the curve of the writing around the root I address that grew into the walls.)

The prison is a deeply inscribed place; I was very conscious of being only the most current of its writings. Civilization tends to be inscribed; the inhabited public landscape is a constant reading, voluntary or otherwise. Islamic architecture wears a web of Allah's praise. Our hortations, though anarchically self-interested, are no less totalizing. The Chinese word for civilization is related to the written. As is our law. Law is a scriptural institution, as in the vocabulary of legal/legible, and generates its counterscripture — my text includes writings found in the prison, often in hidden places. The very identicalness of the cells, by eliminating individuality, seems to bespeak an invisible palimpsest of bodily impressions on them. Writing on walls is often a transgressive act and often associated with those already enclosed as transgressive; to write on a wall of involuntary enclosure seems a gesture of simultaneously territorializing and breaking through or transcending. Place is often property; the one confined to it also. Many of those prison toolings were written as a reverse autograph notched back on the surface of time, a reactive stab of the body subject to the rule that wrote it into there; not so much the large legible slogan, as on the outside, but the secret possession, the voice to a later ear. The legal walls, peeling skinlike, are harmed into whispering the other body back again. Write comes from a word meaning to scratch; scratching digs past the surface; it is a patient, irritant activity for those with time. Seeing whole may not have the time to give to realize that the whole place is about time. And scale. A glimpse saw a festoon. Visual saw writing. Bite-size reading got lecture. Movement and configurations between parties too participate unspoken in laws. Time takes body even if not vice-versa in the "go-to" net. Some of the writing, in its disappearance into darkness, or height, in its scale or even its relentlessness, exceeds reading, as its matter exceeds bodies, and the scale of its matter often exceeds imagining. Including these lapses, these times and spaces of not-reading, the work takes a couple of hours to read, the time of a performance, but there is only the visitor to give moving; and write back out.

Giordano Bruno, whose study of the image led to his discredit by the literal-minded Reformation, elaborated on prior systems of (mentally) superimposing rhetoric on the details of architectural space in order to remember a speech by looking around; he formulated a relation between the visual/spatial, and a system of knowledge. (In my performance work, **YOU–The City**, actors were working to timing but could be interrupted, so memorized their lines according to the spatial point of their journey). Shakespeare's Globe Theatre was an extension of a model such as Bruno's, of the world as coherent, and speakable through seeing. In Frances Yates' writings on Bruno, Fludd and the Art of Memory, illustrations of the Roman circus and of Roman and Elizabethan theatres are an interesting echo of the ground plan of the prison, but with a reverse of focus, the audience in the place of the prisoners, looking in (semi-)circle or long facing rows observing the central "action". Power can be held by being watched as by watching. But it is punishment not to be allowed to move.

Stepping into a cell, despite the open and voluntary entry and any sounds echoing in the corridors, you hear silence, sudden, solid. As much the many silences and solitudes of the place's past as your own. As words fall away there is also compulsion towards them. The cell contains only what is necessary for a human to function physically with minimal humaneness; and that reduced being seems drawn upwards to the source of light, a small round hole in the ceiling. This symbol of release functioned emotionally too: how they made them pray (or go mad). I remembered the very similar, though larger, layout of the cell in the former Trappist (silent) monastery at Ittingen in Switzerland where I had stayed to write a previous book: there the formerly walled garden, just like the separate exercise yard now closed off from each of *these cells, was now open, and the inside door to the cloister where the monks once walked hooded, like this one now door-less to the corridor where the prisoners entered hooded, had been covered. By choice or otherwise, both cut away difference and communication, to a silence of losing person.*

*So in these cells I put photographs. But as of the notion of story in this context, I am wary. Though chapeled off the corridor's nave, these are not icons to keep passive or magical. Who misses a catalogue of faces or atrocites in this book need only look at any Amnesty publication. By now many of the cases I identified the cells with while writing have been replaced, as I followed the Amnesty system of reflecting the ever-current nature of the problem, trying to circulate as many cases into the installation as possible, for public intervention. Aung San Su Kyi was released. Ken Saro-Wiwa was executed. Some demand urgent action. There are always more.*

*ft 96*

# CELLS OF RELEASE

<u>Left side of block:</u>

| | | |
|---|---|---|
| 2. | **Indonesia/West Java**: | tortured for stealing a wallet |
| 4. | **Pakistan**: | death penalty for blasphemy |
| 6. | **Argentina**: | Capuchin monk detained for non-violent activism |
| 8. | **Myanmar**2: | elected candidate for opposition party imprisoned |
| 10. | **Iraq**: | 5 Kurd children "disappeared" |
| 12. | **USA**: | Death Penalty for juvenile |
| 14. | **Tibet/China**: | nuns detained for demonstrating |
| 16. | **Colombia**: | "disappeared" |
| 18. | **Syria**: | detained without trial |
| 20. | **South Korea**: | life imprisonment for "unconverted" |
| 22. | **USA**: | Death penalty for 73-year old woman |
| 24. | **Kuwait**: | life imprisonment for foreigner after Iraqi invasion |
| 26. | **China**: | couple imprisoned for disseminating information |
| 28a. | **Brazil**: | vocal mother of "disappeared" killed |
| 28b. | **Brazil**: | teenagers killed by police |
| 30. | **Indonesia**: | police fatally beat man in hospital |
| 32. | **Mongolia**: | prison inmates starving to death |
| 34. | **India**: | 11-yr old girl raped in custody |
| 36. | **Algeria**: | killed for not wearing the veil |
| 38. | **Uganda**: | mutilation |

<u>Right side of block:</u>

| | | |
|---|---|---|
| 37. | **Bosnia**: | rape as a weapon of war |
| 35. | **Sudan**: | 3 cases — detention, cruel punishment, civilians deliberately killed |
| 33. | **Mexico**: | 3 bodies found in Chiapas |
| 31. | **Myanmar**: | Aung San Suu Kyi's 6th year of house arrest |
| 29. | **Rwanda**: | first woman president—killed in genocidal slaughter |
| 27. | **Burundi**: | political killing of village |
| 25. | **Vietnam**: | recent arrests of Buddhists |
| 23. | **Syria**2: | detained 13 years without charges or trial |
| 21. | **Philippines**: | a victim of police brutality |
| 19. | **Kuwait**2: | "disappeared" |
| 17. | **China**2: | dissidents imprisoned, beaten in prison |
| 15. | **Nigeria**: | human rights activists under fire |
| 13. | **Turkey**: | 13-year-old tortured in custody |
| 11. | **Syria**3: | incommunicado detention |
| 9. | **Venezuela**: | family ill-treated, detained, "disappeared" |
| 7. | **South Korea**2: | long-term political prisoner |
| 5. | **Kenya**: | founder of human rights organization detained |
| 3. | letters **TO** prisoners | |
| 1. | **Sri Lanka**: | released prisoner of conscience T. Kumar |

*For information on Amnesty International, current cases, and letter-writing, contact your local chapter or (in the U.S.):*

*Amnesty International*
*Washington National Office*
*600 Pennsylvania Ave. SE, 5th Floor*
*Washington, D.C. 20003*
*Phone: (202) 544-0200*

# ROOF BOOKS
## Partial List

Recent & Selected Titles

• ECHOLOCATION by Evelyn Reilly. 144 pages. $17.95

• HOW TO FLIT by Mark Johnson. 104 pages. $16.95

• (((...))) by Maxwell Owen Clark. 140 p. $16.95

• THE RECIPROCAL TRANSLATION PROJECT:
SIX CHINESE & SIX AMERICAN POETS TRANSLATE EACH OTHER
edited by James Sherry & Sun Dong. 208 p. $16.95

• DETROIT DETROIT by Anna Vitale. 108 p. $16.95

• GOODNIGHT, MARIE, MAY GOD
HAVE MERCY ON YOUR SOUL by Marie Buck. 108 p. $16.95

• BOOK ABT FANTASY by Chris Sylvester. 104 p. $16.95

• NOISE IN THE FACE OF by David Buuck. 104 p. $16.95

• PARSIVAL by Steve McCaffery. 88 p. $15.95

• DEAD LETTER by Jocelyn Saidenberg. 94 p. $15.95

• SOCIAL PATIENCE by David Brazil. 136 p. $15.95

• THE PHOTOGRAPHER by Ariel Goldberg. 84 p. $15.95

• TOP 40 by Brandon Brown. 138 p. $15.95

• THE MEDEAD by Fiona Templeton. 314 p. $19.95

• LYRIC SEXOLOGY VOL. 1 by Trish Salah. 138 p. $15.95

• INSTANT CLASSIC by erica kaufman  90 p. $14.95

• A MAMMAL OF STYLE by Kit Robinson & Ted Greenwald. 96 p. $14.95

• VILE LILT by Nada Gordon. 114 p. $14.95

• DEAR ALL by Michael Gottlieb. 94 p. $14.95

• FLOWERING MALL by Brandon Brown. 112 p. $14.95.

• MOTES by Craig Dworkin. 88 p. $14.95

•

**Roof Books** are published by Segue Foundation
300 Bowery • New York, NY 10012
For a complete list, please visit roofbooks.com

Roof Books are distributed by
**SMALL PRESS DISTRIBUTION**
1341 Seventh Street • Berkeley, CA. 94710-1403.
spdbooks.org